A Daughter of the King

Kathleen Patricia Perry McKinney Snow

Published by Claire Aldin Publications, LLC
P. O. Box 453, Southfield, MI 48037
www.clairealdin.com

Edited by: Shairon L. Taylor, SLT Inspirations, LLC

All scripture quotations marked (KJV) are from the Holy Bible, King James Version, in the public domain.

Scripture quotations marked (NKJV) are taken from the New King James Version®. Copyright © 1982 by Thomas Nelson. Used by permission. All rights reserved.

Scripture quotations marked (NIV) are taken from the Holy Bible, New International Version®, NIV®. Copyright © 1973, 1978, 1984, 2011 by Biblica, Inc.™ Used by permission of Zondervan. All rights reserved worldwide.
www.zondervan.com The "NIV" and "New International Version" are trademarks registered in the United States Patent and Trademark Office by Biblica, Inc.™

Library of Congress Control Number: 2019931994

ISBN: 978-1-7336560-0-9

Printed in the United States of America

Dedication

In each loss, there is gain
In every gain, there is a loss
And with each ending
Comes a new beginning

~Buddhist Proverb

This book is dedicated to my beloved parents, Ethel Perry and John Colvin McKinney, who are my guardian angels.

To my daughter, Maronica Oglesby and grandson, London Woods: May God keep His angels encamped around you with a hedge of protection from all hurt, harm and danger. May you never be betrayed by the ones you put your trust in and may the love you give others come back to you abundantly. May God lead, guide, and order your steps.

Kathleen Patricia Perry McKinney Snow

ACKNOWLEDGMENTS

I should start by thanking God for blessing me and for the things I have learned in my life. I am thankful that He has allowed me to share some very special things that He has given me to say. This is not my life story, but some of the reflections of my life. God is my lifeline. I lie down, sleep and I wake up again, because the Lord sustains me. I wake up thanking Him for the brand-new mercies and what He has done for me every day. I communicate with Him from the time I open my eyes every morning, until I retire at night. I thank Him in advance for the things He's going to do. I choose to trust God for everything and believe that something good is going to happen for me every day.

To my family: I love you and thank you all for your love and support. Dear Ronica and London, I thank God for you. You have given me two more reasons to live and thrive for an even more productive life. When I tell you "I love you," I'm not saying it just to say it. I say it because you're two of the best gifts of life given to me. I encourage you to always focus on doing the right thing. Don't follow in my footsteps; take your own path and go further. Don't just add Jesus to your life; submit to Him and follow Him. Go where God tells you to go and do what He tells you to do. Be who He tells you to be. He chooses your path. If you feel uncomfortable with what He tells you to do, don't worry about it. He has your back. *"Trust in the Lord with all your heart and lean not on your own understanding; in all your ways acknowledge Him, and He shall direct your paths"* (Proverbs 3:5-6 NKJV). I pray that God surround you with people who will love and care for you. As the world turns, it changes, but God doesn't.

To my sister, Cynceria (Ceri) Wilson, I thank you, especially for all the inspirational quotes you send me daily. It gives me the urge and energy to keep going.

I thank God for the people He has placed in my life to share their points of view. If I tried to thank everyone by name, it would be a while before you get to the next page.

To my readers, I thank you for reading these pages. *A Daughter of the King* is based on Psalm 139:13-24. Hopefully, these words will be an inspiration to you. If I can just reach or connect with one person, maybe that person can reach another one. Thank you again.

~Kathleen Patricia Perry McKinney Snow

☐

Kathleen Patricia Perry McKinney Snow

TABLE OF CONTENTS

Kathleen Patricia Perry McKinney Snow

INTRODUCTION

I have met some very interesting people. I have seen, heard and read so many things that relate to my life. I write of the past and present, and dreams of the future. The power of my future is in the broken pieces of my past. You might be included in my story.

A story is of the past and memories are a selection of images of the past. Behind every person is a story and behind every story is a person. What lies behind us, and what lies before us are tiny matters compared to what lies within us. If you are reading this, you might find yourself in what I have to say. However, if your name is not mentioned, but you are included in these thoughts, you may know who you are. The exclusion of names is to protect the innocent and/or the ignorant.

I was born May 29, 1953 to two loving, strong-minded parents. My mother was a phenomenal woman like no other. It took her only a second to conceive me, and for nine months, she carried me. She gave me life, nurtured me, taught me, dressed me, fought for me, held me, shouted at me and kissed me. Most importantly, she loved me unconditionally. Mama was a "praying" woman. I believe that the essence of my creation is love, which is the greatest commandment. No one should feel that they need to earn love. Love should be automatic.

Did you know that it takes an oyster approximately three years to make a pearl? An oyster can produce multiple beautiful pearls, in any color of the rainbow. Can you imagine being pregnant for three years? If the pearl is mounted on something solid and secured, you can enjoy it for many years to come or for a lifetime.

Mama was still in high school when she had me. Both of my parents worked very hard and instilled in me that I was capable of being whatever I wanted to be. They stipulated that no one was above or beneath me, no less or no more. I didn't have to ask them what I would be or should be. They asked me what I *wanted* to be. As a child, I thought about being a school teacher like my paternal grandmother, a flight attendant or a movie star. My dad told me I was born a star, so I didn't have to try to be one. He always made me smile when he would say that. There are so many women I have looked up to and I used to tell them that I wanted to be just like them. But God showed me how to be me and I thank Him every day for what and who I have become.

I'm just ordinary people. When I look in the mirror, I want to see the goodness of God. God used the kindness of my parents to show me the kindness of the Father. He wins us to Himself with grace and mercy, not with His wrath and judgment. My ultimate dream today is to go places I dream of - travel this Holy Land and set foot where Jesus has been – to follow His path.

Unfortunately, my parent's relationship ended when my dad left Alabama and went to Michigan in his attempt to dodge the Army draft. He lived with Melvin Franklin's family of The Temptations and started working at Chrysler Corporation. There was no escaping Uncle Sam; the Army found him and recruited him anyway. Upon completion of his term in the Army, he returned to Chrysler and retired after 35 years of employment. I was the only child to that union.

My mom birthed five children after me. Three of these siblings have gone home to be with the Lord. My brother, Wayne, gained his wings March 16, 2015. My sister Mildred gained her wings on May 18, 2013 and my brother Lee gained his wings on July 3, 2000. My mom was in the hospital after suffering a second stroke and gained her wings on the day we were burying my brother Lee in 2000. Thank God for my sisters, Sharon and Cynceria, who are living in California.

I am fortunate to also have six of the seven siblings that my other mother, Margarite McKinney birthed for my dad. I don't consider her as my stepmother, but my "other mother." She never treated me like a stepchild. My sister, Tonya moved to her new home in Heaven in November 2009. I am fortunate to still have Johnny, Gerald (Jerry), Katrina, Tina (the glue of the family), Shuan and Dion, all natives of Detroit, Michigan. I am the oldest of 12 siblings, 6 sisters and 6 brothers total. They all have brought great joy to my life as their big sister. I have had a close relationship with all of them. I started to meet my siblings in Michigan at age nine when I took my first trip from Alabama to Detroit for summer vacation. I guess that's when I developed my love of travel. During my visit to Detroit, I went to Canada, which is where I saw my first seahorse. Did you know that the seahorse is the only male species that carries the eggs and babies until they are born? Personally, I guess that's why I only had one child, considering 30 hours of labor and then a C-section. Whew!

I have so many great memories. It is a blessing to have so many sisters and brothers. I see a part of me in all of them. I am my sisters' keeper. I am my sister. Some of my sisters extend my bloodline. I am a sister to all sisters. I am every woman. If given the opportunity to walk a mile in her shoes, I may be able to feel exactly what she has felt or what she may be feeling. I may not have experienced your situation, but I can open my mind to understand or imagine myself in your shoes. I represent my mothers, grandmothers, sisters and other women who have blazed trails, have taught me and walked me through life.

There are not enough words to describe just how important my mother and my father were to me, and what a powerful influence they had on me. My parents both departed this earth at what I consider to be a young age. My dad died at age 60 on January 10, 1995; my mom died at age 65 on July 13, 2000. I truly believe that God assigned them and dispatches them and/or others to be my guardian angels. My dad spent every moment he had with me teaching me about life. I learned so much from him from a man's perspective. I have learned so much from my siblings. Even though I didn't grow up under my dad's roof, I still had a great relationship with him, my other mother and siblings.

I was raised mainly by my mother though my maternal grandmother, Bertha Mae Perry, had a strong hand in raising me as well. I was at my grandparent's house almost every weekend and every other opportunity I got. Some of the wisest teachings came from my grandmother, who had very little schooling. I didn't just grow up; I was raised. I was taught to speak when I enter a room, speak when spoken to, and to say, "Will you," "please" and "thank you." I was raised to respect my elders, lend a helping hand to those in need, open doors and hold doors for the one behind me. I was raised to love people for who they are, not what I want them to be or what I can get from them. I was raised to never judge people. The bottom line is this: Treat people the way I want to be treated.

I remember my grandmother telling me, *"When someone comes at you with their worst, come back with your best."* Former First Lady Michelle Obama said something similar, *"When they go low, you go high."* That has taken a lot of practice for me. Sometimes, people will say things that make you want to knock them into another world, if you know what I mean.

There have been times when I just wanted to set it off with ugly expressions, but I learned to take it to the "Big Guy" (God) and let Him set it off for me. Psalm 46:10 KJV says, "*Be still, and know that I am God: I will be exalted among the heathen, I will be exalted in the earth.*" God has a way of reminding us of the first law of nature, which is self-preservation. We can defend ourselves verbally in a diplomatic way by leaving out the ugly words and not getting physical.

Kathleen Patricia Perry McKinney Snow

Chapter 1

ALWAYS GIVE THANKS

O Give thanks to the Lord, for He is good! His mercy endures

forever.

(Psalm 136:1 NKJV)

In everything give thanks, for this is the will of God in Christ Jesus

for you.

(1 Thessalonians 5:18 NKJV)

We should be thankful and let it be known.

Religious values have always been a big part of my family. I have a deep spiritual outlook and active religious practice in my life. However, I don't live my life by religion, but by my relationship with Jesus. Knowing who has charge over my life makes an ordinary day worth living. This is where my strength comes from. Strength comes from enduring life, surviving the heartaches and agonies while keeping my head held high. Just being able to walk through adversity to get to the other side gives me strength to keep going. I was taught that regardless of your religion, know that there is only one God. Accept His Son, Jesus, as your personal savior and believe in Him. Represent what you believe in. Stick to the gospel. I am weak, but He is strong. He continues to give me strength to endure and live life abundantly. He gives in abundance. He is in my heart and if living is up to my heart, I should live a long time!

I had a far-from-perfect childhood. I have sensed the damage that a controlling and abusive person can do to you. The pain of watching my mother being abused by my stepfather has made me wiser and molded me to become the woman I am today. It feels good to be me despite all the obstacles in my way or the rough patches I've been through.

I realize that your success is not determined by where you come from. Success is determined by what you do. Success requires faith and that can lead you to a desired outcome. Be an optimist and not a pessimist.

Mama married my stepfather when I was five years old. Until I was 14, I witnessed my mom encounter verbal and physical abuse while she was with him. I'm reminded of scenes from *"The Color Purple"* when I picture my mom moving fast throughout the house, scared while looking for things to pack without my stepfather seeing her. She was preparing to go to California when my uncle brought my grandmother back from her visit to California in September 1967. She was a nervous wreck; I can only imagine what was going through her mind. My mother feared my stepfather, not knowing when he would strike and beat her for no apparent reason. He would beat her, and she would not know why. She was a stay-at-home mom who cared for her children. She loved to cook and loved going fishing every chance she got. She was very family oriented.

I knew my Mom was facing her fear of my stepfather when he came in drunk one night with that look in his eyes. When he came towards her, she got the broom and broke it across his head. In the meantime, she also had a pot of water boiling on the stove. She grabbed the handle of that pot and dashed the water towards him, but he dodged most of that hot water. He knew my mom meant business. She took all she was going to take. My mom knew then she'd better pack our bags and catch the first thing smoking to leave Sylacauga, Alabama.

The Color Purple is a movie I can recite practically all the way through. I took my mom with me to see that movie in 1985. She must have had flash backs of what she had gone through. I think she saw part of her life in that movie because she stereotyped poor Danny Glover until she died. Whenever she saw him on television, she would say, with emphasis: *"I can't stand that man."*

I am not where I need to be, but thank God, I'm not where I used to be. What I experienced did not give me the spirit of fear. Instead, it made me bold enough to fight back and become independent. I never feared for myself because my stepfather never whipped me. I felt bad for my mom. I learned to adapt to my environment for that time being. I refused to live in insecurity or self-doubt. I have learned that *fear* is "False Evidence Appearing Real." I fear only God. I know He has my back and He supplies my every need. I truly believe that. He said He would never leave nor forsake me, and never abuse me. I put forth vigorous effort to stay grounded in the Word, though I still fall short. Fear is the opposite of God's greatest tool, which is faith. I choose to fill my mind and heart with the good things of God and those things that have promoted me in a life of *faith:* "Forward All Issues to Heaven". You can't operate or function in fear. Fear can consume you if you allow it.

I am thankful for the ones who have brought me joy and for those who've caused heartache and pain. They have shown me exactly who I don't want to be and what I don't want to do or be a part of. I have learned to humble myself, exhale and respond rather than react. We can't let grudges live rent free in our heads. Don't let people rob you of your enthusiasm. We must learn to respond instead of reacting. If your doctor is treating you for an ailment and you get better, your body is responding. If you start to get worse, you are reacting to the treatment. People can have that same effect on you.

People in our lives have helped us build who we have become. When people try to humiliate you, sometimes the sweetest revenge is success. The way to succeed is to take what was used to break you, and let it make you. Lord, thank you for blocking the things and people who set out to destroy me.

Chapter 2

ANTICIPATE THE POSITIVE

There are people who can point out what's wrong with everyone else, and cannot see what's wrong with themselves. They can see the splinter in your eye but can't see the plank in their own eye. They can point out all your flaws and faults, and yet they are blind to their own flaws. We should sweep around our own door before trying to sweep around someone else's door.

Oh, what tangled webs we weave when we aim to deceive. I've never cared for gossip or critical conversation. *"Let no corrupt communication proceed out of your mouth, but that which is good to the use of edifying, that it may minister grace unto the hearers"* (Ephesians 4:29 KJV). I look for the light and the goodness in everyone and everything. We are all born unique for a reason.

"Happy is the man that findeth wisdom, and the man that getteth understanding. For the merchandise of it is better than the merchandise of silver, and the gain thereof than fine gold" (Proverbs 3:13-14 KJV). *"Say yes to the righteous, that it shall be well with him: for they shall eat the fruit of their doings"* (Isaiah 3:10 KJV). Don't expect others to make you happy because you may end up disappointed. Make yourself happy with the fruit of the spirit: love, joy, peace, longsuffering, gentleness, goodness, faith, meekness, temperance (Galatians 5:22). Opposites of the fruit of the spirit are idolatry, witchcraft, hatred, variance, emulations, wrath, strife, seditions, heresies, envyings, murders and drunkenness.

When I look back on my life, it's not like how Lot's wife looked back and was turned into a pillar of salt (Genesis 19). I look back and reminisce. In May 2017, I toured my old school, Robert Russa Moton High School. R.R. Moton was a segregated school that taught grades 1-12. I visited each of my classrooms. I pictured my teachers' faces and where each of their desks were set up. I pictured some of the faces of my classmates. I remembered some of the fun things we did in class. My first-grade classroom was where I received my first polio vaccine in 1959. As we toured the school, I felt my emotions rise with all the great memories. We also toured the library where I saw paintings of my school principal, Mrs. Corine Patton, and the librarian, Mrs. Gray, who was also one of my teachers.

At the end of my tour, the current principal invited me back for Leadership Day that took place two days later. I was enthused by the students and their ambition. I realized that it's not so much of what you look at that matters, but what you see. Seeing is not believing; believing is seeing. Some cannot see the forest for the trees. There are some who can't see the trees. We should take things at face value and make no more of it than what it really is. All my teachers expected the best of me and I strived to do just that. I was an honor roll student all the years I attended R.R. Moton, and I'm sure that was based on the guidance and expectations from my teachers. I could see that in the students on Leadership Day. In August 2018, I was offered an invitation to be the keynote speaker for R. R. Moton's 11th school reunion by the head of the committee, Mildred Vincent Davis. Of course, I accepted. Having the opportunity to speak on who started us on our educational journey did something for me and to me.

Look for positive in what people do and look for positive in what they don't do. Treat people like they want to be treated. Look at the glass as half full rather than half empty.

Chapter 3

PRAYER OPENS DOORS – JESUS IS THE KEY

The most powerful word that begins with "P" is *prayer*. Prayer changes things and Jesus is the key. The key to heaven was hung on a nail. Jesus chose to be nailed on a cross for us. Prayer is basically just having a sincere talk with God. *"For where two or three are gathered together in my name, there I am in the midst of them"* (Matthew 18:20 KJV).

Prayer brings peace. You can't function in life without peace. You will find annoyance with everything and everybody without peace. You can tell when a person's life is not flowing in peace. When there is a lack of peace, there is confusion. Confusion can't flow if you pray for peace and let God lead. The corrupt human nature has a hostile attitude toward God. The spiritual nature leads to life and peace according to Romans chapters six through eight. Two people can't lead at the same time. One must lead and the other should follow. Whenever two are trying to lead at the same time, it causes conflict. That's like two of you are dancing and you're both trying to lead, or if more than one person is trying to sing lead.

Matthew 16:24-26 tells us how Jesus led His disciples. You must be a good leader to make people want to follow you. I like the story about how Jesus washed his disciples' feet. He modeled what He would have them do unto Him and others (John 13:1-17). What a leader and mentor!

The value of experience is important. We can gain experience through our suffering. Sufferings can equip you to be good and to do good. Doing things your own way can get you in a lot of trouble. Sometimes, we must stop doing

34

what we want to do and do what God says to do. He is constantly trying to promote us, but we can't get the results unless we put forth the effort. We must decrease for Him to increase. We should just ask God, "Will you?", "Please" and say "Thank you" in Jesus' name, thanking Him in advance for the results. For proper deliverance, you must remember to put a stamp on what you send Him, and the stamp is Jesus. God is like a two-way street. You do your part and He will do His part, and it's all through His son, Jesus. All things will work together for the good if you love the Lord and believe. Sometimes, it takes a wrong turn to get you to the right place. God is your compass. Just trust Him and be ready for His power to manifest. If you keep doing what you always did, you will keep getting what you always got. Remove your pride, be quiet, listen, trust and obey (1 Kings 19:11). Most of the time, God speaks in a still, small voice. So, when the teacher speaks, listen.

As Winston Churchill once said, "If you feel like you're going through hell, just keep going". If you've been through hell, don't allow anything or anyone take you back. When someone judges you and constantly criticizes you, just keep going. You will finish strong in the Lord if you just keep going to the word. Don't let them break you or remain in a broken state. Your struggles can give you strength. Pray for guidance and keep moving forward. If you're not going through something right now, you just came out of something or you are on your way into something. Trust God. When you feel like you're at the edge of difficulty, God will either catch you if you fall or He will give you wings. Once you recover, you will become a better you. The Lord will always step in when the devil thinks he's winning.

"I sought the LORD and he heard me, and delivered me from all my fears" (Psalm 34:4 KJV). I love talking to the Lord. Conversations with the Lord don't result in arguments.

There are no worries about discussing what was said. He helps me put what I'm trying to say into words if I ask Him to because He already knows. I have prayed to the Lord to help me put what I'm writing about into words and watched it work. What comes out of your mouth reveals the condition of your heart. However, you must listen before you speak. As a teacher, when you're teaching, you talk; but during the test is when you must listen.

When you've tried your hardest and given it your all, pray and give thanks regardless of the outcome. God always has something new for you to experience. He will hold your hand and lead you to your new encounter. Jesus is our anchor (Hebrews 6).

The sweetest time of the day for me is when I pray because I'm talking to the One who loves me the most. I'm not asking for much; instead, I'm thanking the Lord for all He has done, what He is doing and for what He is going to do. When prayer becomes your habit, miracles can become your lifestyle. Albert Einstein once said, *"There are two ways to live your life: One is as though nothing is a miracle and the other is as though everything is a miracle"*. So, live your life as if miracles are everywhere.

Can you see something without your eyes? Can you feel something, without touching it? Yes, you can. You can feel love and not really touch it. We have eyes yet living in darkness when we can't see what is real about ourselves, about others or about life. You don't need eyes to see God. He knows how to manifest Himself to you in so many ways. Faith is not seen by the natural eye. When we walk by faith, faith can move mountains. If God doesn't move it, He will give you the strength to climb. Faith is the substance of things hoped for, and the evidence of things we cannot see

(Hebrews 11:1). Don't wait to do what pleases God. Keep the faith and please Him now.

God is never far away. He is always with us. When we call on Him, we will always have a divine appointment and opportunities. He may say yes right away; sometimes, He may say no. If He makes you wait, He has a divine reason. Sometimes, God doesn't give us what we pray for. Instead, He may give us the opportunity to obtain it—may it be a new car, a home, riches, patience, courage, etc. When opportunity knocks, open up and let Him in. Do not believe every spirit but test the spirits to see whether they are from God (1 John 4:1).

Faith can create a foundation that we can believe in. Build your faith on the solid rock, not sand. Prayer is one of the best ways to love others. Jesus spent so much time praying

for others. Pray!□

Chapter 4

STEP OUT ON FAITH

When I went to California in 1967, I was 14 years old. All I could pack in one grocery bag was what I could take. We left behind all my school day pictures. Mama stepped out on faith and worked hard to take care of us after moving to California. Mama was quite a lady, and everybody loved her. She learned all she needed to know to take care of her children and keep our heads above water. Not only did Mama raise her children, but she made sure her younger brother graduated high school. Mama worked as a maid for years in the homes of several celebrities. Nowadays, that position is called, "domestic engineer." She knew that if she kept doing what she was doing in Alabama, she was going to get the same results.

If you want something different, you're going to have to break the cycle at some point. Don't lose sight of the Lord, lose your way and fall into the trap of the enemy. If Jesus is your foundation, you are on a solid rock. No matter what your plans are, let Him guide your steps. God will never put more on you than you can bear, or no more than He can handle.

I was always interested in Alabama, where I originated from. My dad and stepmom moved back to Alabama in 1986 when he retired from Chrysler Corporation after 35 years of honorable service. That was a great reason for me to visit Alabama as much as I possibly could. I had been visiting Detroit every year prior to that. My dad tried to catch up on lost time when I would visit, teaching me everything he could possibly teach me about life and love.

I met my friend Jan Porter one week after arriving in California in 1967. She's also from Alabama and eventually went back there to live in 1979. We had lots of fun growing up together and made up for lost time when I would visit her and my family in Alabama. We've been friends for 51 years. In August of 1990, she introduced me to her cousin Henry, who gave me another good reason to visit even more often. He is my soul mate and one of the smartest and most gifted men I know. As fate would have it, he has been a significant figure in my life since I relocated to Alabama in 2006. He has been very near and dear to me through the ups and the downs. He is my hero that does all he can. I am his "shero," the woman who does all the things he can't.

"Alabama" comes from the Choctaw Indian language, "Alabamu," meaning "blazing of the trails," "thicket-clearers or vegetation gatherers." I consider myself a true Alabamian—born, bread and raised by Alabamian parents.

When I relocated to Alabama in 2006, I wasn't sure if I was ready for Alabama or if Alabama was ready for me. I didn't leave Alabama by choice; I was plucked up and taken away. But, as God would have it, He brought me back to where my true roots are, planted and fertilized me to grow to become who and what He has designed me to be. I dare not deny His divine order.

After relocating to Alabama, I would visit my sick stepfather. I asked him why he would beat my mom like he did. He responded, "*I know I was wrong. I thought your Mom was the prettiest woman in the world and I didn't want nobody else to have her.*" I told him, "*Apparently, you didn't want her either because you tried to kill her with the beatings you put on her.*" He just dropped his head and said, "*I was wrong.*" I don't know if my Mom forgave him, but I forgave him for her. He passed away in 2013. God rest their souls.

God wanted me to get planted and to thrive in every season of my life, no matter what the circumstances were. I endeavor to find victory in my daily challenges, reach higher, dream bigger and believe all of God's promises. Dream big dreams and with faith and confidence in yourself, you can accomplish the goals that God have placed in your heart. Visualize yourself rising to new levels of effectiveness. God's favor begins with your faithfulness.

Set out to make each day as amazing as God has designed it to be. Look for the best in every minute. Open-minded people embrace being wrong, don't mind admitting it, apologize for it and question everything, even themselves. Out of respect for yourself and others, don't refuse to see or admit what you're doing wrong. There is favor in doing the right thing. God helps those who help themselves. It's up to you. Don't allow pride to corrupt your relationship with God or others.

Kathleen Patricia Perry McKinney Snow

Chapter 5

THE GREATEST LOVE OF ALL –

RELATIONSHIPS

Love is the most powerful thing on earth. There is no greater force than love. Life is all about love. If you start to share it, I believe you will find that there is enough to go around. God shares His love every day through the sun, the moon, the stars and even the rain, which I call "liquid love."

From a wise woman's point of view:

First, love yourself. There is only one you, so love yourself to death. If you can't love you, how can you expect others to love you? I've heard some say that "a piece of man is better than no man at all." I disagree. My philosophy is a piece of a man is not better than a whole, healthy man. Why settle for less? If you don't know how to love me, maybe you're just not ready to learn. I am willing to teach you how to love me if you're willing to learn. But I really believe if God wanted you to raise a man, He would have given you a son.

I've also heard it said that when you meet the love of your life, time stops because your heart skips a beat and when it starts again, it beats overtime. How do you know if your heart is strong enough? Some think that if you never give your heart, you can never get it broken. That's a fear of falling in love. I remember when I "fell" in high school. When we graduated, John Oglesby, Jr and I got married and our daughter Maronica was born, which gave us a permanent bond. Our marriage resulted in divorce but we are still friends and keep in touch to this day.

I hope you find what you're looking for; however, jewels are to be *sought*. Diamonds or the finest gold doesn't make a woman. A divine woman is a gem—a precious stone, especially when cut and polished. We are worth far more than that according to Proverbs 31. "Divas" are women with divine, inspirational and virtuous attitudes towards life. A virtuous woman may be broken down temporarily, but she knows how to rebuild herself and come back strong. Sometimes, what you're looking for could very well be behind you. If you slow down long enough, love will tap you on your back, turn you around and embrace you. Recognize it and embrace it back.

Don't allow an earthly man to validate you. Allowing a man to define who you are as a woman leaves you open to being controlled and eventually abused, either physically, mentally, verbally or both. Never give up hope. Hopeless people are easily controlled. Sometimes, words can hurt more than a punch. Like a match, the tongue can strike and burn (James 3). You've probably heard the quote, "Sticks and stones may break my bones, but words can never hurt me." I disagree with part of that phrase. Words can break your heart. Harsh words can sting like a bee and unlike the wasp, the bee leaves its stinger. You will need to remove the stinger before you feel some relief, but pain and discomfort will linger, sometimes for days. The memory can linger forever. You will never forget how it made you feel. The damage is done.

We can break each other's hearts with the words we say. It's called verbal vandalism. There is a right way to address any issue. Some people know just the right things to say. Some neglect to engage their brain before putting their mouth in gear, and out comes the negative, derogatory or hurtful words than can leave a permanent scar. Don't be corrupted by the poison that's spat out at you. The longer we hold on to it, the deeper the resentment and bitterness grows. We can't live with poison inside us. What poison is in your life?

It takes a real man to know that a loyal woman is one of the greatest things he can have in his life. A real man doesn't hurt his woman. He doesn't make her cry from hurt. If he does, remember God collects your tears. His woman is to be loved and protected, not used and abused. Love does not reject or neglect you. Love does not dismiss or ignore you. Love does not deny you. However, if you lash out in anger or frustration, be prepared to receive the same in return. Even the gentlest person can take only so much of a crazy attitude. Sometimes, we must adjust the attitudes. Our attitude towards our Heavenly Father determines our attitude toward each other. What you believe and the way you think affects what you do, how you respond or the way you may allow yourself to feel. Attitude has everything to do with it. Reciprocate what you want and expect it.

I've never been beaten by a man. I never got a whipping by my father, my stepfather, grandfather or uncles, so I dare not accept being a recipient of a whipping by any other man. God doesn't even whip us. We whip ourselves with the repercussions of being disobedient. Don't even entertain the thought of giving a man that kind of power regardless of how much he does for you.

Blessed is the woman who has her own mind and abilities. We need to handle our business financially, educationally and spiritually. Don't compromise your moral values. Being with a man who does not have your best interests at heart tends to chip away at the very essence of you. When you let someone chip away at your heart, you may have nothing left to share with someone who truly loves you. Listen to your instincts; they usually don't lead you wrong.

Be careful who you vent to. Some listening ears have running mouths. Keep your comments about your mate to yourself, even if you're tempted to talk about it with a family member. Many relationships have been broken due to a family member putting their two cents in or fabricating what you said. That's a prime example of a peace breaker. If that so-called friend or family member is unhappy, they want everybody else to be unhappy. If they are hurting, they tend to hurt others. I've been there and experienced that. Guard yourself, your heart and your mind from gossip, negativity and unhealthy associations. Don't be distracted from peace and positivity.

If you want to be treated like a queen, behave like a queen. You must carry yourself like royalty. A queen settles for nothing less than loyalty, and a man who treats her that way. If you don't like the way you are now, then change. Life doesn't get better by chance; it gets better by *change*. If it has taken you a lifetime to get the way you are, it will take more time to understand and remove the negative effects of your life. Your storms won't change unless you change. Humble yourself and let God in. *"Be ye transformed by the renewing of your mind..."* (Romans 12:2 NKJV). You have a choice.

Do not give in to fear, ignorance or hatred. Fear can paralyze you. If you feed into hate, hate only wears you down. Jealously usually opens the gate to hate. A strong woman doesn't seek revenge, she lets God do the work. Watch God move.

Sometimes, you must experience a bad relationship to really understand what a great relationship is like. One man's nightmare can be another man's ultimate dream. One man's trash is another man's treasure. What one might throw away can be a seed of an abundant harvest for someone else. What you throw away may still have value. Why is it that some men constantly seek rhinestones when they have a diamond (a virtuous woman) in their hand? *"Who can find a virtuous woman? For her price is far above rubies"* (Proverbs 31:10 KJV). A woman is a jewel. Jewels are not to seek; they are to be sought.

Diamonds are formed by pressure. You are just a diamond in the rough that can be chiseled and shaped to perfection with kindness, joy and love. Surround yourself with other jewels. Some men may think that a woman wants him for his car, his money or gifts, but a virtuous woman only expects his time, his smile, his honesty, his efforts and putting her first. Because her true Man, Jesus, provides her every need, she wants for nothing. If you're rejected, don't feel bad. The one rejecting you don't recognize value, so they don't deserve or can't afford you anyway. They can only love you to the capacity they truly love themselves. Only God can supply your life with the riches you really need.

I believe that I am a strong, wonderful, beautiful, powerful, humble, lovable and fabulous woman. Believe these things about yourself and accept that it is true. When you are told these things by everyone except your man, there is something wrong with that picture. Check your "male." Some men are intimidated by that many qualities in one woman. It's hard for some to recognize a jewel. They can have a diamond in the palm of their hands and they are still searching for rhinestones. If you're not worth his hand in marriage, so be it. Know when to walk away. It takes a strong person to walk away.

Don't focus on what you've lost. Focus on what you have to gain. If you lose someone because you're not perfect enough for them, but you find yourself, you've won. Don't try to be perfect for imperfect people.

I support marriage. You must learn how to be married. Whatever you do to get them, you must do to keep them. You must be a walking representation of what marriage is. Don't let others cut the fabric of who you really are. When you are building a strong marriage, the enemy will throw twice as many obstacles your way. God will command blessings in unity. Your union will be blessed.

Favor increases with unity when it's no longer mine or yours, but *ours*. Don't be led on. Some of us may be content with a boyfriend/companion, and some would love to settle with a husband. What would Jesus have you do? If you have a true husband, he is your prince and you are his princess. If you're not married, your prince is on his way. Consider what is best for you in the long run. Remember, you are the daughter of a King. Keep your trust in Him and things will always fall in place.

Communicating your interests is important. Even if you disagree on some things, it's not the end of the line and not the end of your world. Learn how to turn self-interest into mutual interest. It's good to have different interests. However, you then have something to share and discuss.

To all the single ladies and single mothers who are working hard to make ends meet, your prince is on his way. Be grateful for your children, for your job and for life. If you're not sure what's lying beside you right now, you may be better off by yourself. Even the eagle flies alone. Sometimes, being alone can be better than being with the wrong one. Be ready to receive God's goodness and the one He sends to you. If you stay ready, you don't have to get ready. You were created for more than this moment right now. You will receive everything according to God's promise by the power of His Word. Just meditate on it. Keep the faith.

Let go of what's holding your life hostage. Don't let anyone bring you down to their level. Release them from the hold they have on you and continue with peace in your heart. Life is too short to waste precious time trying to figure them out or prove anything to them. It's pathetic how much time we waste on certain people and in the end, they prove they weren't even worth any of it. Holding on to bitterness and anger will only hinder your growth and your happiness. You are much too precious to spend your time worrying about someone that brings you bitterness. Strive to be the best person you can possibly be. Be strong. You don't need a "Superwoman" cape to still be amazingly strong. Prove to yourself and everybody will see. Say goodbye and wish them well. This should make you stronger.

Don't accept someone who constantly puts you down. Be the bigger person. Life is too short to waste your time with anyone who doesn't appreciate you. You are valuable. A woman's heart is like a vault. Once you're in, you're in; once you're out, you are out. Make Jesus your groom, lover and savior. Don't stay stuck in a relationship that's not going anywhere. Keep moving forward. Believe in second chances, but there may be no next time. Sometimes, it's now or never. Treasure each moment and utilize it wisely. Even if you lose everything, if you still have God, that's enough to start over.

Oftentimes, what you thought was your greatest loss can be your greatest blessing. God gives second chances and can make things new. Don't be afraid to try something new. Take the next step. In most cases, those who try to tell you what you should do, could do, dictate how you should live your life or how you should raise your children are usually unhappy people. They have skeletons in their closet that they will never reveal to you. They need to get a life of their own and stay out of yours.

God sees your value when people don't. He is the one who validates you, not people. Don't minimize yourself to make insecure people feel better. God gave you His Son and He is awesome. Some seek to find the worst in others, but God sees the best in you. Try to avoid getting involved with such people. They will smile in your face and stab you in the back while hugging and patting you on the back.

God can calm any storm in our lives and that's what we expect of Him. He wants us to see Him in the storm and dance in the rain. He is in every situation, even the ones we have no control over. Stop looking at the storm and look at the miracles of God. He will keep you going even when you want to give up. He provides us with what we need to weather the storms of life. I believe all of His promises.

When you have problems with your mate, and can't agree on anything, you need to explore the root of the problems. Problems are multiplied if you don't examine the root. You can't get to the bottom of the issue by jumping all around in a no-nonsense conversation. Get to the point without putting so many layers on it. Otherwise, it is not a conversation but instead, bad communication. Stay on one topic until it's settled. Handle one thing at a time. Let your conversation be gracious and attractive so that you will have the right response for everyone. Let your speech be seasoned, so that you may know how you ought to answer. Good communication develops comfort and is the key to breaking barriers. The heart and mind don't always listen to each other, but if you examine the issue, you may reach a happy medium. Whatever you are feeling, you don't have to pretend with God and He doesn't pretend with us. God has a way of making our feelings clearer when we open ourselves up to Him. He will broaden our understanding if we give Him a chance.

We must make rational choices in our relationships. We must pay attention to each other. Don't compete with each other's success. Success should be shared with your mate. Make healthy deposits into relationships. Keep putting love into it. Be spontaneous. Don't allow people to suck the life out of you with negativity. Is your relationship nourishing or is it toxic? Does it drain you or does it build you up? Pursue people of purpose—God's purpose. The person we think is our type may not be who God wants for us. Things and people are not always as they appear. If your mate is doing or giving all the things *they like*, that's the opposite of how it should be done. You should be doing and giving the things the *receiver* likes.

Have you ever been in a relationship you know you shouldn't have been in? You probably thought it was a good idea at the beginning, but it wasn't a "God" idea. You may have to be the bigger person and walk away to avoid confusion. Remain friends and love that person 'til death do you part. Don't become enemies. Absence can make the heart grow fonder.

Seeing is not believing; believing is seeing. Seek someone you can trust and can talk to about everything, rather than someone who wants to talk only about themselves or someone else. People need different things. Do whatever you have to do to get to the point where you can trust and be trusted. Remember, God sends people to you for a reason. There may be a lesson in it for you or for them. You may be able to help or teach each other along the way. Most people are good people. You must be able to get to the core of who they really are and let go of the judgment. Align your thought before going into the action. Think about an alignment on your car. If your tires are aligned, you can save tread and add miles to your travel.

Whoever you choose, make sure you agree on beliefs and desires, but don't disqualify yourself. Whether it's your mate, friend or family — give what they need rather than what you want to give them. Ask necessary questions. I might need something at the bottom of the mountain, but you want everything at the top. People may stop loving us, but God won't. That's one thing we can brag about: God's love. God never fails. We are to die for because Jesus died for us. So, let's live for Him. People will judge and condemn us, but God won't. You may hear people say, "I used to love him or her," but the truth is, if you're grounded in love, it doesn't go away. We don't want watered-down love.

Don't try to hold on to something that is not aligned with God's Word or His will. Even seasons know exactly when to change. Have you noticed that the "Dogwood" tree has been blessed to bloom just in time for Easter? The most unique part of the tree is that the petals are formed in the shape of a cross. Learn your own seasons. There's a time for everything (Ecclesiastes 3).

As stated earlier, love can be felt without touching it. Love doesn't start with your eyes, it starts with your heart, which is where love is housed. Your heart should be the best part of you. It's easy to love when you come to understand what love is. Love the people that God gives you—your family, children, friends, associates, co-workers. By God's grace, we are made for one another, to take care of each other. We are God's family. It may not be easy to love a stranger, but you may be entertaining an angel. You might say, "I just don't like that person" and the last thing on our mind is loving that person. But, if you don't have it in you, you can't give it out.

God gives us gifts for a reason. Do not ignore your gift. Your gift is the thing you can do your best at with the least amount of effort. When you are thankful for your gifts and use them, your gifts can bless you and others. Grace is one of the greatest gifts. Show grace and mercy to others. Grace is the power and ability of God operating through us. When God sees you doing your best at developing and building what He has given you, He will do His part and open doors that no man can close. You do your part, and God will do His. Be genuine to yourself and treat others in such a way so they'll know you are genuine. Let them see the God in you.

Love is the only thing that matters. If we each practice due diligence, you can't help but love one another. If you have done something you wish you never did, don't take it out on others. Don't get stuck in the pain of the past. That can ruin your future. Your past is gone. Don't relive it. Let it go and move on. Don't take what happened to you out on others. No one should have to live out the sins of anyone else. Never allow yourself to feel persecuted or scorned because of what happened in someone else's life.

I'd like to share what I have learned about relationships, whether it be your mate, family or friends. A healthy relationship requires willingness: First and foremost, a believer and doer of the Most High.

- Focus on what you have in common

- Practice being pleasurable

- Actively listen to what you're hearing or saying

- Treat each other equally

- Spend quality time together

- Be supportive of each other's ideas and dreams

- Trust

- Be encouraging

- Give mutual respect

- Be accountable

- Honest and open communication

- Always express your appreciation and kindness

- Embrace each other through your adversities

- Laugh together

These things should come naturally; however, you may need to work on them. Be willing to compromise. The following are the opposite of any of the above, and they are unhealthy.

- Blaming your partner for everything, never taking the blame for our own wrong doing

- Ignoring others' feelings

- Being disrespectful

- Using the silent treatment

- Only one of you makes all the decisions (has control)

- Isolation from friends and family

- Trying to control the other person.

Lack of love creates problems. Love does not judge. Don't try to change people. If we could change people, we would be changing them for our benefit and it takes away their freedom to be themselves. We all should be able to make our own choices. We must be willing to work on whatever is going wrong. Perfect love costs you nothing. The perfect love casts out fear (I John 4:18). Perfect love is love

70

unconditional, that "agape" love, which is the greatest love of all.

Kathleen Patricia Perry McKinney Snow

Chapter 6

BE WHO YOU ARE DESIGNED TO BE

Know your own self-worth. Stop measuring life and appreciate it. There is nothing in this world that could equal the value of the temple that God has given you. So, don't put a price tag on yourself. If you want to label yourself, the label should say "God's Property." Regardless to your ethnic cultures growing up, you can create your own culture by the way you recreate yourself. We all have a platform. This world is God's stadium and we all have a part in it. Don't stop living before you stop living. There is always someone whose life can be positively impacted by the way they see you, and you may not be aware of it. Our influence is so important to those around us. They watch us constantly to make sure we walk the walk and not just talk the talk. We must constantly ask ourselves if we are a good role model, especially for our children. You may never fully realize the impact you have on others.

During my first through eighth grade school years in Alabama, my teachers and my classmates would always nominate me to run for everything. Of course, my mom was most encouraging. Mama would help me bake cakes and I would sell cake slices for 10 cents. I would make popcorn and sell small bags for five cents and large bags for10 cents. She bought boxes of candy for me to sell. I sold cookies for one cent each. If Mama caught any fish during the week, we cooked and sold fish sandwiches on weekends.

I was homecoming queen in first, third and fifth grades. I was "Ms. Cafeteria" in sixth grade, which was the year my school built the cafeteria at Robert Russa Moton High School in Sycamore, Alabama. I was always given the longest vocal part in all the school plays. Mama took me to the seamstress to get fitted and paid for my costumes to be made.

In California, I attended Bret Harte Junior High School, George Washington College Preparatory High School and I graduated from Alain Leroy Locke College Preparatory High School. I majored in theater, with a minor in music at Southwest Community in Los Angeles. I also attended John Robert Powers Modeling School. I started out modelling hats for "Alberta Turner and the Mad Hatters." I later attended Webster Career College to enhance my business skills and later graduated with honors.

I never had the fear of poverty and I didn't know what poor was until I reached adulthood. I learned the meaning of survival and independence at a young age. I strived for higher education in every sense of the word. I have never been afraid to share my intellectual side or my knowledge. I have never been afraid of setting my standards high. A liberal education can free a person from their own prison, how they think. Think of freedom not as the right to do what we please to do, but as an opportunity to do what is right. I grew up with an independent mindset and I wanted to pursue my own career. I am thankful for the struggles I've endured. I have looked for reasons or tried to make sense of why bad things happen to good people, such as illness, injuries, rejection and disappointment. *"I will lift up mine eyes to the hills from whence comes my help..."* (Psalm 121:1 KJV), and I thank Him for I know He has a divine purpose for all things.

I have progressed from the pain of struggle. I am so thankful that my weaknesses helped me focus and strive for strength in those areas of my life. I needed to experience my past to get me to where I am today. My past helped me to set a course of direction that motivates and drives me to excel rather than allowing it to hold me back. The Lord allows things to happen and everything happens exactly when they are supposed to happen. God has the answer to my every need. At this point in life, God is the only One I answer to. He is present wherever I am. I praise Him every moment, through happy times, difficult times, quiet times and painful times.

I believe that I was made in His image. Each day is a gift from Him and He is in control of every moment. Just because you don't see Him doesn't mean that He's not there. One time, we were in church and the pastor said, "The Lord is real, He is in the house today," My grandson, who was about four years old at the time, said in a loud voice, "If He's real, why can't we see Him then?" The following Sunday, the pastor had all the children come to the front of the church where he demonstrated with a glass of water and a sponge. He sat the glass of water down and asked what was in the glass. They all answered, "Water." He then took the sponge and inserted it into the glass and the sponge soaked up all the water. That was a great way to make them realize that just because they couldn't see the water didn't mean it was not there. Again, seeing is not believing, believing is seeing.

Trust your gut when God gives you insight, when you feel something is wrong. Trust your feelings. Be the authentic *you*! There are no shortcuts to authenticity. Be who you are, not what someone else wants you to be. Other people's perception of you is their business, not yours. You know who you are. It's up to them to learn who you are. Know your strengths, weaknesses and your limitations. Don't let others put limitations on you. Life happens!

Why would you want to be like someone else and deny your own uniqueness? We should never want to be anyone else.

You may admire certain qualities of others, but you want to be the person God created you to be. I can't think of anyone else I want to be like. My sister Ceri once asked me why I didn't pursue a career as an actress. I told her that if I had, I would be spending my life being someone else and not who God designed me to be. When you are comfortable, you are not growing. So, don't get too comfortable. Sometimes, we must step out of our comfort zone. Never be totally content. Don't be content with good when you know you can do better. Be the best at being you.

Be ready for a new conquest. You might experience some growing pains, but it's up to you to make it worth your pain. There is always room for improvement. We should work on improving ourselves every day. If you are not happy with who or what you are, then change. Don't wait for someone else to change. Change yourself. Go forward, letting go of what is behind, including past mistakes and past victories.

The world will keep turning whether we're here or not, so put forth your most vigorous effort to live a productive and joyous life. Don't live your life focused on the rearview mirror, thinking of all the things you wish you had done. The past doesn't have to destroy or poison your future, so let's start doing something about it right now and focus on going forward. Getting started can be tough, but if we could just put ourselves in gear, we just might be unstoppable. You may not have a college degree, but if you have God's *decree*, you are covered by His grace, and there is nothing impossible for you. Declare what God has for you and live it. *"Thou shalt also decree a thing, and it shall be established unto thee: and the light shall shine upon thy ways"* (Job 22:28 KJV).

We must correct the wrongs and get rid of the excess baggage for God to work. Don't associate with people who are gossipers and have negative attitudes. Surround yourself with those who can strengthen your weaknesses.

I was born an artist, and my life is an unfinished painting. I have dropped the brush several times along the way, but I knew I had to finish at some point. Like a planted seed, my roots hit a rock and stunted my growth, but the soil has been cultivated and the season is now, and it's just right for new growth. In other words, I am starting where I am. I had to determine if what I've wanted to do could be done and find the way and time to get started.

Being an optimist and a spiritualist, it's only natural for me to share with you past and present life experiences. I hope that it helps you or someone you know along the way. I want to share what I've done to get over stumbling blocks and get rid of excess baggage. I have learned to not be a bag lady. I shake the negative thoughts in my head to my shoulders, shift them to my feet, build a mental bridge and step over it. Don't allow yourself to become a dumpster and carry the weight of excess baggage.

When trash overflows in your home, what do you do? You need to empty it. If you want to fly, you must give up stuff that weighs you down. You'll eventually get tired of dragging that load around. Give your excess baggage to God and thank Him for taking that heavy load off you. Don't put lugs and weights on your heart. Jesus is your heart anchor.

When you recognize your gift(s), pursue it with passion. Pursue what you're passionate about and use your key to happiness. All of us are not multi-talented, but we are all gifted and we all have at least one talent. So, make a smart choice, pursue and build on your dreams. Live your dream and not someone else's dream. Be careful who you tell your dreams to. There are people who will try to live your dream for themselves. You can always tell your secrets and dreams to the Lord; they will always be safe with Him. He is your diary. He is the One who gives and allows our dreams. When disappointment or rejection knocks you down, get back up and try again. Sometimes, taking a different route in the right direction can take you where you need to be. Don't give up on your God-given dreams. Don't throw away confidence; it will be richly rewarded. We need to persevere so that when we have done the will of God, we will receive what He has promised (Hebrews 10:35-36).

"No weapon formed against you shall prosper" (Isaiah 54:17 NKJV). I made a commitment based on Isaiah 54 that every offering I contributed for the year 2017, my check will be for $54.17. There is a miraculous meaning to my method. *"If God be for us, who can be against us?"* (Romans 8:31 KJV) The Lord is willing to take every negative thing that has happened to you and turn it into something positive if you're willing to believe. I believe that God has an awesome plan for me and for you. Receive, believe and become.

I am encouraged to show love to all who cross my path. When we display positive behavior, there is always someone who can be impacted in a positive way that we may not even realize. Say things and do things in hopes that you will have a positive impact on their life. The Scripture says that a generous man will prosper. Commit yourself to encourage and make it a daily goal. He who refreshes others will himself be refreshed (Proverbs 11:25 NIV). Choose happiness as a main goal. Stay focused on your goal. It's easy to lose sight of your goal if you allow distractions to overwhelm you. Be so happy that when others look at you, they'll become happy, too.

God is the designer of my life — past, present and future. He sets my goals. I thank Him every day for all He has done. I thank Him for my pain and for my disappointments. I have learned from my painful situations. I had to break old habits to clearly see my gift and new talents. I choose to close the door to certain parts of my past to get through the doors that have opened for me. I can't carry excess baggage with me. I took a deep breath and stepped into my purpose. All things work together for good (Romans 8:28 NKJV). I know where I came from, but only God knows where I'm going. He laid my path and my destiny is set. My steps are ordered by Him.

God's plans for my life shall come to pass. He is all-powerful and allows all things that happen. Nothing happens without His will. He is just and fair, and He stands for people getting what they deserve, so that the good prosper and the wicked are punished (Isaiah 3:11). I'm not a firm believer of luck. The word "luck" is the term used by non-believers for "blessed." Luck is a way to try to explain things without including God in it. I haven't found "luck" in the Good Book. Everything is connected to something and God's hand is behind everything. There are no incidents or accidents. I work at replacing that word with "good fortune/fortunate."

I am not a preacher, but I can see how God has used my experiences to help me to minister to someone today who may be lonely or hurting. It is effortless for me to find some encouraging words to anyone who feels alone, lost or hurting. I can be changed by what happens to me, but I refuse to be reduced by it in any sense of the word. Don't mistake my silence for ignorance, calmness for acceptance, or kindness for weakness.

Robin Williams once said, "The worst thing in life is to end up with people that make you feel all alone." There is a difference in being alone and being lonely. I thought the worst thing in life was to end up alone, but it's not. Some people feel better off alone because they have been hurt or bruised. *"The righteous cry, and the Lord hears, and delivers them out of all their troubles"* (Psalm 34:17 NKJV).

"Surround yourself with thinkers and doers. Great minds discuss ideas, average minds discuss events and simple minds discuss people," said Maya Angelou. And for you liars, the truth will set you free as soon as you recognize the lies that are holding you hostage. The truth will make you free if you're consistent and tell the whole truth. Don't add to or take away or remove any part of the whole truth. Evading the truth or stretching the truth is just as bad as lying. I know someone who has told the same lies over and over until those lies became the truth to them. Anyone who can't come clean knows nothing about the truth. It's possible that they are afraid of what they'll find while searching themselves for the truth.

I refuse to allow any human being to sit high and look low to judge me. It's not man's job to contain me or try to overhaul me. That's God's job and He doesn't need any help with that. Everyone has a chapter in their life they don't read out loud. In other words, everything is not public information. There are some things that you and the "Big Guy" (God) should discuss in private. Be you and have your own relationship with God.

As the late, great Maya Angelou so eloquently stated, *"When someone shows you who they are, believe them the first time."* Don't fool yourself to think that people are just reacting to you. What they're really doing is being who they really are. Have you heard the saying, *"A drunk mind speaks a sober heart"*? When they show you the real "them," be the real "you." When you feel like you're under attack, you are under performing for the devil. Attack is of the enemy. People will often attack you because they fear you or feel intimidated by you. When people come against you, humble yourself therefore under the mighty hand of God, that he may exalt you in due time. Come under the hand of God (1 Peter 5:6). To reach your divine destiny, you must live in an active partnership with God, obeying His instructions.

My quiet time is from about 2 a.m. to 5 a.m. I have my best conversations with God during that time. That's when I clearly hear God speaking to me. One morning, He said, *"You are trying to hold on to something that wasn't aligned with my Word."* I knew just what He was talking about. Just because this is the way you want to do things does not make it the right way. You need to get out of your own way. Don't block your blessings. Let go and let God.

When people don't understand your views or your life, maybe they never will and really don't need to. Just because your views are different doesn't make you a fool. You may have done foolish things, but it doesn't qualify you as a fool. Realizing that our life is worth something to us should also allow you to see that the lives of others are just as special. Some may think that their life is more important because of how much money they make or how much they may have. Your life is not their journey and it's not their destiny. No two directions are ever the same. The road of life has twists and turns. Our lessons come from our journey and everybody's destiny should be in the direction of heaven. If you run into a dead end, it's not a dead end if it's somewhere you're supposed to be. Not all roads lead to heaven, but He will put the right highway in front of you "just like that," if you believe. So, if you're in the driver's seat, move over. If you are the pilot, switch seats. God is your pilot and Jesus is your co-pilot. Welcome to acceptance and enjoy your journey.

When you have the rain and the sun appearing at one time, that's your chance to see a rainbow. The rainbow is a promise from God (Genesis 9:13-16). Make yourself happy. If you depend on someone else to make you happy, you may be very disappointed. Happiness should be your main goal if what you're doing makes God happy. Everyone deserves a little happiness in life.

In all honesty, I can always find something I did, said or thought that was wrong. That's why it's so important for me to stay in the Word to help me get grounded and stay grounded. When I started attending weekly Bible study faithfully, I learned so much from my pastor. I love being able to ask questions for clarification to help me better understand. If you want to see me kicking and screaming, try to keep me from Bible Study.

When I was in elementary school, the teacher would whisper something into a student's ear and ask that student to pass it on. When it reached the last student, it was something totally different. Either someone didn't hear it correctly or someone didn't repeat it correctly or both. That's how rumors get started. Imagine that! That's one of the reasons I don't like to talk about people unless it's Jesus because I can read what's true for myself in the B.I.B.L.E. — "Basic Instructions Before Leaving Earth." I serve One who I can tell anything to and He won't tell anybody. If you don't know Him, I would like to introduce Him to you. You will never want to cut your ties of communication with Him.

I cannot allow every little thing I hear to enter my reality. What I hear, I don't always absorb, but there are some things I need to hear. However, I am learning to become a better listener to only what is important. If what I heard enters my realm and I find later that it bothers me, I must shake if from my head to my shoulder, shift it to my feet and move on. I call that "building a bridge and getting over it."

I took a ceramics class in my 10th grade year at Washington High School in Los Angeles, California. I would take a mound of clay, put it on the wheel and spin the wheel at the right speed to form and shape the perfect pot of clay. I loved the idea of my hands being in the wet clay as I tried to perfect a vase, a flower pot, a soup bowl, a coffee cup or a sculpture. At the end of the semester, I would bring my creation home to use it or put on display somewhere in our house. I believe when I'm doing right, God smiles on me. I am reminded of the story about the potter's wheel in Jeremiah 18. I imagine myself being that clay in the Lord's hands and it makes me smile. I don't always do the right things, so I can only imagine how He must feel because He's not only trying to make me good, but He's trying to make you good as well. I know His job is not easy.

"Do not give dogs what is sacred; do not throw your pearls to pigs. If you do, they may trample them under their feet, and turn and tear you to pieces" (Matthew 7:6 NIV). As Jewel Diamond Taylor once said, *"Don't let everybody breathe on your baby."* In other words, do not waste good things or time on people who will not appreciate them. You can't share your dreams or your visions with everyone. Don't let anyone tell you what you can't do or what won't work for you. Just because someone is in your life doesn't mean that they want the best for you. You make your own circle. To succeed you must not allow others to control your destiny. Let your heart lead you and stand up to the fear of displeasing other people. Know that you are a child of a King and you need no other validation.

Things don't automatically happen. Faith is required to succeed. Faith is your greatest potential and it must be developed and used to see your dreams manifest. I have hope for my dreams and visions, as well as yours. May you see them manifest. You must work at being a better version of *you*. Life doesn't get better by chance, it gets better by change. If you are not happy with who you are, take a chance, and make a choice to make a change for the better. If you keep doing what you have always done, you will keep getting what you're getting, or you will always be what you've always been.

Keep the faith in God. Find your passion and decide. Lack of self-motivation can stunt your growth. Focus on yourself and not others. Ask yourself how you feel about your life. It shouldn't matter what anyone else thinks; is it what you want it to be? If not, find fulfillment. It's your choice. Sometimes, you may have to be your own coach. Never limit or underestimate God's power. Pray for guidance. The key is being willing to listen. Act when He speaks and follow His lead. As the Serenity Prayer goes, *"Lord, grant me the serenity to accept the things I cannot change, courage to change the things I can, and wisdom to know the difference."* Life may be cruel, life may make you sad, and life may make you want to hurt someone. No matter how hard life gets, you are never alone. Life is full of so many possibilities. Always look for the beauty in life. Life can be beautiful.

If we have breath, then we still have purpose. God has a purpose even for our struggles and hurt. Faithfulness is what He admires the most. He is never late, but never early. He is always right on time.

Inside you is where you live. You take you with you wherever you go. Everything you do, you do it with you, so be the best *you* can be. What's inside you is what comes out. Don't give up on you. Don't expect anyone to rescue you from you. Rescue yourself and do what the Lord say do. Go where the Lord say go and be who the Lord say be. Be what He has designed you to be.

If you could find your name in the dictionary, what word defines you? What would it say about you? What would be your description? Some of us may even find our names in the Bible but we don't necessarily live up to the characters defined in it. Think about it! How do you define yourself? What does the way you carry yourself say about you, your character, and your attitude? Self-inventory may help you understand, determine, and define yourself. The best of your life is yet to come. *"Whoever pursues righteousness and love finds life, prosperity and honor"* (Proverbs 21:21 NIV).

Kathleen Patricia Perry McKinney Snow

Chapter 7

ACTS OF KINDNESS

CARING FROM YOUR HEART

AND NOT YOUR HEAD

You may feel that you are the only one putting forth all the effort in your home, in your relationship, whether its family, friends, spouse or mate, but that's okay. You may always be the one who initiate all the phone calls. You may the first one to say, "I love you." Everyone should want and appreciate that "You're okay?", "Thinking of you," "I miss you" call. But everyone can't be you. They may never initiate that kindness because they don't know how. You can't give what you don't have, so we shouldn't expect anything in return. Just keep doing what you do and make each day as amazing as possible. You will see what's so amazing about grace. Show affection. No act of kindness—big or small, is ever wasted.

A smile and a good attitude can mean so much. When you see someone without a smile, give them yours. Usually, you'll get one back. A smile can add value to your face. Jesus has the best attitude and is the most positive thinker I know.

You should want to be in the lives of people who want you in theirs. You want the ones who accept you for who you are and not what they want you to be. You should want to be in the lives of those who would do anything to see you happy and who loves you regardless. Desire someone who is there for you whenever, wherever. Don't expect everyone to give you credit for what you do. Just keep doing your best. Whatever you do, do it from your heart and just be happy you were able to do it. It's all about helping people.

Being happy does not mean always getting what you want. Happiness is when you love what you do, what you have and you are grateful for it. Start by doing something simple and exhibit an act of kindness to those around you. You may become a role model for someone. You may even find a role model in the least expected place and at the least expected time. We all need a role model. Satan can't have your joy unless you give it to him. Don't let Satan become your role model!

My heart is driven to visit and help the sick and shut in. Whether they are in their home or in a convalescent home, I will cook for them, feed them and do whatever they need done or can't do for themselves. I like to give flowers while they can still smell them and enjoy the beauty. I will run errands for them. I love to sit with them and listen to their stories. Being around the elderly gives me a better perspective and makes me strive for stronger faith, wisdom and knowledge. Conversations with them make me focus on having a more solid foundation of faith. You know that your Heavenly Master will reward all of us for whatever good we do. What you make happen for others, God will make happen for you (Ephesians 6:8). We reap what we sow (Galatians 6:7-9).

Chapter 8

LIFE IS A TEST

We are all tested. As you go through difficult times, pray against temptation and all forces of darkness. Those things are meant to distract you from God. God will stand by you and the victory will be yours. God tests us all the time to see if we're ready to go to the next phase of life. A test is a challenge to see if you're willing to go through the process to get to the next level of life. Tests are necessary and make you appreciate life. Tests are lessons that strengthen us if we don't give up.

Tests give you experience and ultimately become your testimonies. Testimonies can empower you to help someone else by sharing the tests you've passed, your trials and triumphs. I've dealt with a great proportion of crises, and I have decided to get out of my own way, out of the way of others and out of the Lord's way so He can do what He wants to do.

Make each day as amazing as God has designed it to be. It's up to you. He gives all of us 24 hours in a day, so it's up to you how you utilize that time. As Mamie McCullough puts it, "*Yesterday is a canceled check, and tomorrow is a promissory note. Today is the only ready cash you have to spend, so spend it wisely.*" Life may not permit us to go back and fix what we've done wrong, but it does allow for us to live each day better than yesterday. Welcome opportunity and take advantage of every opportunity. Sometimes, opportunities may rise when you least expect them. If you stay ready, you don't have to get ready. Do what you're supposed to do in the time you have; we only have one life to live.

Sickness is a test. Humbling exposure through pain is good for the soul, believe it or not. It's one of the ways God instructs us as sinners in His ways. Humility guides us in what is right. God tests our faith, our patience, our temper, our weaknesses and our beliefs. God tests your temperament. It takes a stronger person to walk away from a situation than to stay and fight about something that's not worth it. Don't let temperamental issues ruin your life. We are proof of God's patience. Just think about what He has put up with waiting on us to do the right things.

God is putting things together, so we don't regret a moment spent culminating, growing and going through our tests (Romans 8:28). Taste and see that the Lord is good (Psalm 34:8).

A person thinks everything he does is right, but the Lord weighs hearts (Proverbs 21:2). Ponder, consider and review. Everything you have gone through is a test for your next best assignment. I've learned from my trials and tribulations and I know who cares and loves me the most.

Patience is a test. God will always answer us faithfully. Sometimes, His answer to our questions is a much desired "yes." Sometimes, His answer is "no." He may even make us to "wait." When it seems that you get no sign or answer, that's when He is simply saying, "Trust Me." Remember, He is an on-time God! God has a way of setting you up. He will test your faith to see if you are ready to move to the next level. Be ready for your promotion. He is the only one who can promote you in every area of your life.

Chapter 9

IT'S NOT WHAT YOU DID,

IT'S WHAT YOU DIDN'T DO

In mid-February 2017, I was suffering with sciatica nerve pain that had me basically bedridden for almost a week. The medicine I took had no positive effect. Whenever I got up, I had to walk bent forward to ease the pain. I walked with a cane for approximately three weeks. I spent my time in bed reading the Bible and other inspirational books that described my own talents and experiences. God has a way of flipping you on your back to make you look at Him. As I lay flat on my back, I clearly heard God speak to me, saying, *"You have a gift; now it's up to you to use it." "For the Lord giveth wisdom; out of His mouth cometh knowledge and understanding"* (Proverbs 2:6 KJV). I knew clearly what this meant and was very perceptive to what I was ordained to do. I was so inspired, I decided to share my own memories. That's when my journey began.

This is the day I chose to close the door to some things in my past. I chose to start my walk step by step into my present and open the doors to my future. I believe that what is possible can be possible to me if it's for me. Your talent is God's gift to you. What you do with it is your gift to God. To reach your divine destiny, you must live in an active partnership with God and obey His instructions.

You must think beyond where you are, or you will never go beyond where you are. Broaden your way of thinking. Read the Prayer of Jabez in 1 Chronicles 4:9-10. Enlarge your territory and increase your impact. Attempt something large enough that failure is guaranteed — unless God steps in. Pray this: *"The Lord is my shepherd, I shall not want"* (Psalm 23 KJV). He will always rise to defend His sheep.

God will get to you what belongs to you, but, if you don't believe, you won't see it. He will give you what you need. God will break the stronghold that the devil may have on you. You win! When the devil tries to lead you to the dark, use that light of yours and let it shine. Jesus gave you that light. Walking in the dark without light can be hazardous. People who do what is wrong hate the light and don't come to the light. They don't want their actions to be exposed. But people who do what is true, come to the light so that the things they do for God may be clearly seen (John 3:20). Darkness and light can't exist in the same place, at the same time. Night time is the only time we see the stars. Let the brightest light guide you. Jesus is my Star.

I started to share my story about 20 years ago, but apparently, I wasn't at the fullness of who I really am today. I told myself that my someday will begin today. By grace and mercy, I am a survivor and a conqueror. I am a born nurturer, caregiver with a strong sense of ethics, morals and values. It's not difficult to say, "I love you" or to say, "I'm sorry." You can't give what you don't have. If you don't have it in you, you can't give it out. You may have done something or said something you regret. Reconciliation starts with forgiveness. It takes a real man or woman to reach out, step up and say and do the right thing. Learn to quickly say "I'm sorry," "forgive me," "I love you." It takes maturity to apologize, even when it's not your fault. Apologize and let it go for the sake of peace. I reiterate, if it's not in you, you can't give it out. Do what you expect others to do for you. *"Blessed are the peacemakers, for they shall be called children of God"* (Matthew 5:9 KJV).

There are people who will always blame others instead of themselves. Lord, forgive them for they know not what they do. You must forgive whether you're asked for it or not. That's where the healing begins. What is in you is what comes out. I have been around people who just don't know how to express love. To truly love others, you must first love yourself. Loving and being in love are two different things.

As I mentioned previously, I love a challenge. I like to set at least three goals a day for myself and I challenge myself to reach them. If I reach two, I'm good. If I reach all three, I've completed what I set out to do. Where there is no challenge, there is no change. Where there is no change, there is no growth. The purpose of a driven life is a life of driven purpose. I don't want to just go through life, I want to *grow* through life. There is no doubt that through life, we will experience conflict and stress. We have choices to accept the things we cannot change, courage to change the things we can and wisdom to know the difference, which is my daily prayer.

Sometimes, we should coach ourselves to persevere. We must program our minds to pursue the best in life. If we are not programming our own minds, believe me, someone else is. There will always be one to take what you say or do, and try to con you into thinking or believing the scenario set in their minds. What they need to do is do what they do, and not scandalize or vandalize your ideas. If what you're doing is good, they will tell nobody, and if it's bad, they will tell everybody.

We may fail, but it doesn't mean that we have failed life. Humpty Dumpty fell off the wall and all the king's horses and all the king's men could not put him back together again. They were calling on the wrong king. I know a King who can mend broken pieces. How do you restore a broken heart?

I'm sure we all have scars that are nowhere near the surface of our skin. You may be able to lead a heart to love, but you can't make it fall. Some may think if you never give your heart, you can never get it broken. Some are just not very good at love because of the fear that's embedded from a past relationship. As Mama used to say, *"Nothing beats a failure but a try."*

God will promote you at the right time. He can make grace abound so that we will have all that we need and will abound in every good work. When God gives you something and you don't use it, you lose it. Everything we do should be for the glory of God. When you are done, He will say, *"Well done, my good and faithful servant."*

My past has helped me understand the present. I will not drag my past with me, but I think back and I thank God for His grace and mercy. I'm not quite where I need to be, but I'm not where I used to be. I am a woman with a mission. When I accomplish one mission, I'm off and running to my next. I consider my missions as divine assignments. I have been told that God gifted me to be a divine, inspirational, virtuous and anointed woman. I like to spread these traits everywhere I go. I am not a very religious woman, but I am very spiritual. Falling in love with Jesus was the best thing I've ever done.

It's not always what we do that create hurt, pain or misunderstanding. Sometimes, it's what we *don't* do. What we don't do can change a person's life and leave it void of the small things that could bring the biggest smile and happiness. It may be just a kiss on the cheek, a touch, or three simple words: "I love you." It may be a phone call when you're away to say hello and to see how they're doing. The best feeling is when someone can appreciate everything about you that someone else takes for granted. When their arms are not opening to receive you, they are literally pushing you away into the arms of another. Jesus' hands are always outstretched, and His arms are always open wide to receive you, and embrace you with warmth and care to lead you in the right direction.

It's important to know the love languages of the people we care about. I recently read "The Five Love Languages" by Gary Chapman. The five languages are: *Words of Affirmation, Quality Time, Acts of Service, Physical Touch and Receiving Gifts.* A gift doesn't have to be extravagant to be appreciated. It's the thought that counts. I gave this book and audio package to my brother Shuan when I attended his wedding in Michigan recently. Shuan and his bride, Charlene, considered the gift as a confirmation. They said that their pastor counselled them on marriage from this book and each week, their pastor would ask if they had purchased the book. Of course, the answer was "not yet." They were surprised when they opened their gift from me. We need to take note and analyze what's missing in our relationships with our mate, our children, our friends and family. Ultimately, our relationship with God is what determines our relationships with others.

I love and care for someone very near and dear to me who struggles with Alzheimer's disease. Her husband is her primary caregiver and treats her like the queen that she is. As I sat and talked with him one morning, he said to me, *"Patricia, I have asked God, what have I done to deserve what I'm going through with taking care of my wife?"* I asked him, *"Did He answer you?"* He said, *"No, not yet."* As I sat and thought about his question, the answer came through me. I remembered he once told me that he and his wife's biggest disagreements were because of time. She felt he never had enough time for her, being dedicated to work as head of a unanimous business, which included meetings and travel. When I brought that to his attention, I told him that I was instructed to remind him that, "*It wasn't what he did, but what he didn't do.*" I told him that she didn't have the time she felt she deserved once upon a time, but now she has him 24-7. He said, "*I wish I had as much faith as you.*" I squeezed the tips of my thumb and index finger together and said, "*I only have the size of a mustard seed,*" and that's all you need.

Chapter 10

SOMETHING IS MISSING

When something is broken, you don't necessarily have to get rid of it. Don't allow yourself to be trapped by a broken situation or circumstance. Invest your time and effort to get what's necessary to fix it. If you want something bad enough, you will do what's necessary to fix it and hold on to it. You may give out but don't ever give up. If you give up, you stop proving yourself to *you*. Prove to yourself and everyone else will see.

Not too long ago, I told someone I consider very near and dear to me that I loved them. Their response was, *"You don't love nobody but yourself."* During a dispute with this same person, I called "Jesus" and was told that I should be ashamed of myself for calling Jesus into this mess. I have no problem bringing Jesus into my turmoil. I don't want Jesus missing in my life. Personally, I don't think there is a wrong time to call Jesus. Jesus is the greatest lover of all. He has the greatest personality, He has the greatest wisdom and the greatest understanding. He is the greatest doctor and lawyer. He is all of that and more.

My Dad would always say to me, *"Tricia, how is it you attract so many people? You don't meet strangers."* As it says in Hebrews 13:2 KJV, *"Be not forgetful to entertain strangers: for thereby some have entertained angels unawares."* I've learned to surround myself with positive people. I consider myself a people lover and a great communicator, but I don't want to surround myself with negative people who dampen my spirit, ridicule my ideas or desires. I try to surround myself with people whose strengths can enhance my weaknesses. I have learned to attach myself to those people or things that gets my gift in motion. I don't listen to the voices of people that pull me down. I gravitate toward people of a higher caliber. However, I have made mistakes and found myself in those negative surroundings, but only for a short period of time. Bad company corrupts good morals, so choose your friends wisely. Don't let friends choose you. I didn't rehearse my mistakes, thinking about what I can't do or how I didn't have what it takes to move forward. I've refused to let my mistakes make me. I've decided to live my life free from the accusations of the enemy.

I have paid close attention to people who can take a comment or a situation and decipher the positive and those who dwell on the negative or only see the worst in people. There are some who seek to find the worst in people. Try to avoid getting involved with people like that. That can bring you down and can drain the positive energy if we allow it. Proverbs 13:20 KJV states that *"He that walketh with wise men shall be wise: but a companion of fools shall be destroyed."*

I'm sure all of us know someone who will always give you a negative answer when you ask, *"How are you today?"* You'll always get some type of negative response. I have learned to just say "Hello" to some people, without asking how they are doing. Sometimes, you may still hear a bit of negativity, but I have learned to respond with a positive gesture like, *"Just believe that things will be greater later."* Some people are always having a bad day. Choose to surround yourself with people who are always looking forward to brighter days, those who are expecting something better and doing what can be done to make it happen.

There is a difference between expressing issues in life versus constant complaining. Stop complaining and act positive towards the situation. Regardless of the situation, do something to make the situation better. Such negative effects can be very damaging to a relationship. Small adjustments may avoid a fight, which is a mark of love. Put your ego down and think positive!

It's not in tough times or sorrowful situations only when people need encouragement. We need to make a daily effort to encourage, energize and inspire someone. I love to hear other people's thoughts or opinions although I may disagree sometimes. When you allow the Lord and positive thinking to be your guide, it is amazing what your outcome can be. People with positive attitudes sees the light of the situation. On the other hand, people with negative attitudes only see the dark side of the situation. What makes all the difference is how we think. As a man thinketh in his heart, so is he. A positive attitude has something like a magic effect. Be ye transformed by the renewing of your mind. If you don't like who you are, it's up to you to make some changes (Romans 12:2).

We should stop trying to impress people. Don't worry about other people's opinions. God never told us to impress people, only to love them. We don't necessarily have to like them or like their ways, but we must love them. Making everybody else happy is not in your hands, but making *yourself* happy is in your hands. You can evaluate the people in your life and decide who you want to promote, demote or terminate. You are your own chief and our CEO is the Almighty. Sometimes, it is too late to rewind. You must reset, and sometimes, you should just delete.

If you catch a fish and realize it's too small, throw it back. A fish grows when it doesn't get caught too soon. Hopefully someone else will catch it in due time and be happy. Would you rather be a big fish in a small pond or a smaller fish in a larger body of water? That may depend on your potential to grow.

Someone asked me why I always had to be in the limelight? My response was, "*I was born with this light and this little light of mine, I'm going to let it shine.*" You are light for the world. A city cannot be hidden when it located on a hill. No one lights a lamp and puts it under a basket. Instead, everyone who lights a lamp puts it on a lamp stand. Then its light shines on everyone in the house. In the same way let your light shine in front of people. Then they will see the good that you do and praise your Father in Heaven (Matthew 5:14-16). My light never goes out because the One who gave it to me determines when it goes out and stop shining.

It took me a while to realize it, but that person was the one who wanted to be in the limelight. Obviously, they wanted me to dim my light, so they could shine a little brighter. They couldn't handle my light. If someone really loves you, when they see that light, they should want to shine with you. I won't dim my light to fit into someone else's life. I just use what God has given me. I use every gift I have. No one can strip me of the gifts and talents God has given me. I have a lot more to give. I guess that was the way they were dealing with themselves. I thought to myself, "*Whether you love me or hate me, I'm still going to shine.*" I just prayed and I lost no love for them; however, I couldn't dim my light. I just had to share with them how they could increase the voltage on their own light.

When people don't understand what you're doing and why you're doing it, they tend to falsely judge you. There is always that someone who is trying to sit you down, because they don't want you to be heard or noticed. They want you to forget about who you are designed to be and sit in a corner. I don't think so, I'm not her, okay? There is a legacy for me to leave behind that was discovered with this little light. What they had to realize is that they were not the one who controls my voltage.

That person finally learned how to control their own voltage. They were taking notes all along. I guess my light was just too bright for them. They started wearing sunglasses! *"Thy word is a lamp unto my feet, and a light unto my path"* (Psalm 119:105 KJV). I understood their criticism, so I prayed. *"And when you stand praying, if you hold anything against anyone, forgive them, so that the Father in heaven may forgive you your sins"* (Mark 11:25 NIV).

Life is not about being rich, popular, highly educated or being perfect. You can have a degree and not know how to do what you spent years in school for. Someone must lead you, and hands-on training is the best tool. No one knows everything. On a different occasion, that same person told me, *"You think you know every damn thing."* The problem is that I knew something they didn't know or had an idea that worked, and that bothered them. My response, with attitude, was, *"I don't know every damn thing, but what I know,*

I know it well." I don't claim to be tough, but a piece of leather well put together.

Do you know someone who's critical and always have something negative to say? Always judging and analyzing others, jumping to negative conclusions, slandering other people's dreams and ideas? They focus on fabrication to bring demeaning views on others. We need to boost morale, not deflate it by putting negative tags on someone who doesn't deserve it. No one deserves it, but it happens all the time.

Some of us are missing out on the good things about a person because too much time is spent analyzing and pointing out the worst about someone. Tell someone, "You can do it!" or "Good job!" I choose to look at the positive.

Statistics show that women are verbal and more apt to express true feelings and men internalize and hesitate at getting to the point. Communication is fundamental for a healthy relationship. If you have no communication, you have no meaningful relationship. You must talk about things and talk from the heart. Men internalize and hold on to situations from the past, for weeks, months, years, and try to bring them into the present. That's excess baggage. That baggage should have been unpacked way back then. Don't struggle with baggage that weighs you down and gets in the way of progressing. Emotional baggage is only going to bother you and the only one it's going to hold back is you. So, let it go.

You can tell the tree by the fruit it bears. We should all bear the fruit of the Spirit. Like branches on a tree, we reach in different directions, but the fruit it bears is determined by its roots. Practice at looking for the beauty and strength in people, not their flaws or their weaknesses. Point out their beauty, uniqueness and strength instead. Iron sharpens iron. The more you see your own flaws and sins, the more precious and amazing God's grace will become to you.

Chapter 11

INSECURITIES

If you compare yourself to others, are jealous of others and their passions or abilities, or trying to keep up with everybody else, you are insecure. Insecure people criticize everything that's different from what they would choose. Insecure people are usually uncomfortable when they are not on their own turf because they are not the one in control. They are the ones with the competitive edge who will always try to keep ahead. You can tell them what you're going to do, and they will beat you doing it or try to top your idea. They will always try to make you look small, less than, or beneath them to make themselves appear bigger than or more than you. This attitude falls under the true definition of insecurity.

Some people have no idea who they really are because their identity is centered around themselves. They have no clue of what's happening outside of the life they live. They will use whatever is necessary to make themselves look good or dominate any situation. They are constantly feeding their own ego, so they associate only with people who cater to them. Otherwise, they feel betrayed. These people tend to feel superior if they can do something others can't. What they don't understand is that God gives everyone grace and favor to do what He assigns them to do. I am sure they're good at something that you are not. *"As each one has received a gift, minister it to one another, as good stewards of the manifold grace of God"* (1 Peter 4:10 NKJV).

Protect yourself from this kind of personality disorder. They are constantly dishing out insults, condescending remarks and flies off the handle at the slightest disagreement. I've been around people who exaggerate or deliberately lie about their achievements, and when they talk about work, hobbies or relationships, all you hear is how much they do, how great they are, and how lucky people are to have them in their lives. They feel they are the undisputed "star." They expect you to always go along with their demands or ideas. That's selfish!

We all have some personality disorders. My issue is that I tend to speak the truth, and some don't handle that very well. It actually pisses some people off. At that point, I pray for favor and hope they know that I meant well. I don't purposely do or say things to hurt feelings. Speaking has been one of my greatest gifts and I'm always asking God to give me favor, direct my lips and allow the right words to flow so the receiver interprets them in a positive way.

When someone loves everything they do, but criticizes everybody else, always suspicious or look for ulterior motives in other actions, that's an insecure person. If we spent as much time minding our own business and analyzing ourselves, maybe our circumstances could be better. You can miss out on the fun things in life and the beauty in people when you try to analyze everything and everybody. When someone only tells the bad or derogatory stories about a person, there is really something they like about that person. They won't talk about what they like, but only what they don't like about that person. Avoid people who want to silence your personality and criticize you for being yourself. Avoid those who constantly find something wrong with everyone you know. These are insecure people. They don't like it when you exercise your mind. Some are just inclined to see only what's wrong. Think about the story of Job in the Bible. He took it all and waited for the goodness to be revealed to him. Today, we would consider that as torture.

I remember being criticized for encouraging others in the church congregation to read the Bible in a year based on the Bible guide. I was shocked to be criticized about something like reading the Bible — the Word of God. I just summed it up that this was a person trapped in a cocoon with a limited way of thinking and that's why they criticized my suggestion. I prayed that God would give them a new heart and a new way of thinking. *"A new heart also will I give you, and a new spirit will I put within you: and I will take away the stony heart out of your flesh, and I will give you an heart of flesh"* (Ezekiel 36:26 KJV).

John 1:12 NIV says, *"Yet to all who did receive him, to those who believed in his name, he gave the right to become children of God."* Believe it or not, I have seen this same person transform before my eyes and has become more interested in the Word. Thank you, Lord. "Believe=Receive =Become." Believing is the key to receiving.

Don't be afraid of being judged or criticized. That's what haters and insecure people do. Love your enemies and haters. Do good to those who are jealous or hate you. Bless those who curse you and pray for those who mistreat you. *"Mockers resent correction, so they avoid the wise. A happy heart makes a cheerful face; but heartache crushes the spirit. The discerning heart seeks knowledge, but the mouth of a fool feeds on folly"* (Proverbs 15:12-14 NIV). We can't allow such ridicule to keep us from fulfilling what we have been designed to be. How can you stand out if you're like everybody else? Be your authentic self. Reach beyond your boundaries, connect with people different from you and utilize their strengths to build on your weakness. Don't ever disqualify yourself and don't allow others to disqualify you. Always be prepared to advance. We can't control what people think or say but we can control us. Your words and actions will tell the whole world who you are. There is always room for improvement so just continue working on being the best you can be.

A satisfied life is better than a successful life, because success is measured by others based upon what you have achieved. Our satisfaction is measured by our own soul, mind and heart. Be successful at being you, not someone else. It's time to soar with eagles rather than pecking around with chickens. If you associate with successful people, before long, their enthusiasm will be contagious. If you stay in an atmosphere of victory, you will develop a winning mindset. If you hang around people of faith, your own faith will increase. You won't know the outcome unless you start. Discipline yourself, be consistent, plan and work at it. Form good habits and set your goals.

Avoid people who belittle you or your ambitions. Insecure and small-minded people do that, but great people make you feel that you can become great. Great minds have purposes, others simply have wishes. Friends are those who help us and encourage us do what we can. A book is like a friend, but does what no friend can do—stay quiet when you want to vent, or you want to think.

We need people in our lives who have love for the Lord and are willing to learn together and to get a revelation. However, I do understand that we all must live up to our own expectations. Don't give up when it gets hard for you. Just keep believing. *"It is better to trust in the Lord than to put confidence in man"* (Psalms 118:8 NKJV).

"Keep thy tongue from evil and thy lips from speaking guile" (Psalm 34:13 KJV). The tongue can be a fire. It can corrupt the whole body like a weapon of destruction. *"Depart from evil and do good; seek peace and pursue it"* (Psalm 34:14 KJV). *"Let your speech always be with grace, seasoned with salt, that you may know how you ought to answer..."* (Colossians 4:6 NKJV).

Begin everything you do with this affirmation: *"I will succeed."* Determine if the thing you want to do can be done and then find the way. Learn your purpose in life. Ask God and He will reveal it to you if you're really seeking Him and expect it to manifest. Seek His wisdom. Most locked doors are only in your mind. You must first put something or someone good into your life if you expect to get something or someone good out of it. Whatever you focus on the most is magnified, and you give strength to it. So, focus on the positive. Give your strength to God's purpose for you. Keep strife out of your life. Whatever you do, do it with excellence (Isaiah 13:7-8).

A NOTE ON DEPRESSION

Don't allow yourself to be overwhelmed, manipulated or depressed because of issues in your life. I have researched that as much as 85% of depression or sadness leading to depression is caused by life's most stressful situations and the most common are[1]:

- Loss of a loved one, loss of a job, loss of a friendship, loss of financial security

- Holding in anger

- Difficulty in being productive

- Improper perspective on life

- Improper priorities

- Fear of aging and dying; loneliness

- Guilt

If you have recognized the fact that you are depressed by any of the above or even something else, it's not a matter of life and death. Recognizing and admitting to it is a good thing. Some people can be depressed and are the last to recognize it. There are so many ways to get help.

My grandson blames a lot of his downfalls on depression. He dropped out of University of Alabama during his third year because he said he was depressed. He had been out of school for a while before he shared it with the family. I urged and encouraged him and encourage anybody else to get help. Small things can have the greatest impact on one who is experiencing depression, but you don't have to suffer. I urge anyone to confront the situation by doing whatever you need to get help. Make it a matter of life, not death. Though the Bible doesn't use the word "depression," it refers to similar words such as "downcast," "mournful," "brokenhearted," "troubled," "miserable" and "despairing."

There is nothing new under the sun. It's new to us because this is a different time. If you go off on the deep end, who do you expect to go overboard behind you? Pray about it and believe that God will see you through it all. This too shall pass because He is a "miracle worker."

Here are a few key principles I adapted years ago which may be able to help control stress and depression. It's okay to talk to yourself and tell yourself:

. I am human like you and will not be ashamed of me

. My needs and desires are important to me

. I am a person of worth

. I appreciate myself

. I will promote myself spiritually, mentally and physically

- I will only be friends with those who respect me because I am valuable

- I will not live up to anyone else's standards

- I will express my uniqueness, as I can be no other

- I will not try to meet other's demands to prove my self- worth

- I will determine what is essential in my life and what is not

When Satan points out my weaknesses, I will praise the Lord who understands and helps me with my weaknesses. You can try this whenever you are feeling depressed.

Kathleen Patricia Perry McKinney Snow

Chapter 12

THE HEALING POWER OF ANGELS IN THE OUTFIELD

(Hebrews 13:2)

One of my favorite movies is "Angels in the Outfield." Believe in angels and hang out on their wings. Just know that they are with you. The thought of angels brings joy and happiness. They are there to catch our tears when we cry, no matter how hard we cry. Sometimes, we may hold in a lot, like when we're down and out, in pain and don't want to bother others, so we hold our tears. Our tears fall when the heart just can't handle the pain just like the rain falls because the clouds can't handle the weight. A cloud doesn't fall, it releases the pressure.

Angels exist in heaven, or the spirit realm, which is a level of existence higher than the physical universe. God created the angels through Jesus, whom the Bible calls "the firstborn of all creation" (Colossians 1:13-17). The Bible gives names of only two angels, Michael and Gabriel (Daniel 12:1; Luke 1:26). I don't know if God calls all of His angels by name, but we have the liberty of naming our own angels.

I believe that angels have distinct personalities and communicate with one another. They have thinking ability and able to compose expression of praise to God.

Angels are used by God as He directs His servants in preaching of the good news of the Kingdom of God (Revelation 14:6-7). This will benefit both those preaching and those hearing the good news. Angels help to keep the Christians free of contamination of wicked people. (Matthew 13:49). Although angels look out for the spiritual welfare of

God's servants, this does not necessarily mean that God assigns an angel to each Christian as personal guardian (Matthew 18:10). Angels do not protect God's servants from every trial or temptation. The Bible tells us that God will often "make a way out" of a trial by giving a person the wisdom and strength to endure. Angels fight alongside Jesus Christ to eliminate wickedness (2 Thessalonians 1:6-8).

"Do not forget to entertain strangers, for by doing so some have unwittingly entertained angels" (Hebrews 13:2 NKJV). You may never know when you've been greeted by an angel. I will never forget the day in Texas as I awaited my connecting flight home. I was on my way back home to Alabama after spending the last 10 days of my sister Mildred's life in California. While there with her, I made her laugh with childhood stories. I was there to help bathe her, pamper her, massage her ailing body, dress her and encourage her to recognize God's voice because she already

knew He was calling her home. When I arrived at her house, she asked, *"Pat, what are you doing here?"* I said, *"I am here to see you."* She said, *"You should have waited a few days longer."* After she died, I knew what she meant by that statement.

When I landed in Texas, my cell phone was filled with missed calls and texts from my sister, Ceri. When I called her back, she told me that I needed to come back to California because Mildred had gone on to be with the Lord. She told me to just go to the ticket agent because my ticket was already taken care of to return to California and to call her when I got a confirmation. My flight left at 7 a.m., and Mildred died at 7:30 a.m. While sitting at the airport in Texas in tears, I asked God to guide me, help me quick, and tell me what to do. Two little old ladies (angels) came up to me to comfort me and asked what was wrong as I sobbed. I told them what I was experiencing and one of them said, *"The Lord will answer you."* That supernatural experience led me to an even closer relationship with God. Angels show up in the strangest places and at the darkest hour. They wear so many faces.

In a matter of minutes, as I sat in the airport in Texas waiting for my connector flight and waiting to hear from God, I clearly heard a strong, masculine but gentle voice over the intercom saying, "*Keep going Patricia. You were there when she needed you, I have her now.*" I looked at everyone around me, who all appeared to be oblivious to what I heard. They all continued with their cell phones, tablets and computer activity. I knew right then, that was the answer to my prayer. God had spoken to me. I called my sister Ceri back and told her that I had a confirmation. She asked when I would be arriving back in California. I told her that I had a confirmation from God and what He said to me and she said, "*I understand.*" When I made it home to Alabama, we made flight arrangements for my daughter to go to California to fill in the gap. It's all a memory now.

According to Maya Angelou, *"People will forget what you said. People will forget what you did, but people will never forget how you made them feel"*. Sometimes, we don't know the value of a moment until it becomes a memory. I realize that we are all born to die, but I encourage you, don't think about dying, think about living. *"And He will send his angels and gather his elect from the four winds, from the ends of the earth to the ends of the heavens"* (Mark 13:27 NIV).

I'm reminded of a terrible accident that one of our associate pastors experienced in 2017. He was T-boned by an 18-wheeler and ejected from his vehicle. He said he could feel himself soaring and didn't remember hitting the ground. It appeared that angels caught him with their wings and laid him to the ground without a scratch on him. However, he did experience some internal concussions, but is doing fine.

Play like there are no winners, give like you have plenty, love like you'll never be hurt, and try as though you've never failed. Dream like you believe in miracles, love life like it's heaven right here on earth. God sees, hears and knows it all. Dance with the angels. Keep a smile on your face, your eyes on God and a song in your heart and He won't allow you to fail.

For the Believers:

"May the Lord cause you to flourish, both you and your children. May you be blessed by the Lord, the Maker of heaven and earth."

(Psalm 115:14-15 NIV)

"All scripture is given by inspiration of God, and is profitable for doctrine, for reproof, for correction, for instruction in righteousness." (2 Timothy 3:16 KJV)

"Have mercy on me, O God, according to your unfailing love; according to your great compassion blot out my transgressions. Wash away all my iniquity and cleanse me from my sin." (Psalm 51:1-2 NIV)

"I am the Vine, you are the branches. He who abides in Me and I in him, bears much fruit; for without Me you can do nothing." (John 15:5 NKJV)

You can identify with every woman. I think it gives you longevity. Women, you can be the woman that every woman can connect with and every man should be able to appreciate. Women do more than just birth babies. They bring joy and hope. They are compassionate and encourage us to be better. They give moral support. When God made woman, the world was changed forever. He knew what He was doing when He made woman. Women are the most mysterious of mankind, but this is where you will find beauty and wisdom, strength, intelligence and charm. Real men like that in a woman. I pray with hope that each of your experiences will point you to God.

Lord, thank you for your divine purpose and order. You brought me through that and I know You will bring me through this, and I'm so grateful to You. I know I have been pre-approved for all the blessings you have for me and I'm thanking You in advance.

I am thankful for all the writers and my teachers in my life. You have helped to shape my life. Every experience and every person have carved an impression of me. I don't want to go back to any part of my life because I wouldn't know then what I know now. I focus on moving forward.

END NOTES

1. McCullough, Mamie. *I can. You Can Too.* Nashville, TN: Thomas Nelson, 1987

PATRICIA, A DAUGHTER OF THE KING

FAMILY PHOTOS

Mama

Stepmother

FAMILY PHOTOS

Daddy

FAMILY PHOTOS

Me and Mama

FAMILY PHOTOS

Me and Daddy

FAMILY PHOTOS

From top left to right – Wayne, Mildred, Patricia, Nathaniel

Lee, Ceri, Mama, Sharon

FAMILY PHOTOS

Siblings from left to right – Tonya, Johnny, Jerry, Dion,

Shuan, Patricia, Tina, Trina

THE MANY FACES OF PATRICIA

Grade Six at R. R. Moton

High School – 1971

THE MANY FACES OF PATRICIA

40th Birthday

THE MANY FACES OF PATRICIA

50th Birthday

FAMILY PHOTOS

Maronica, Patricia, and London

Kathleen Patricia Perry McKinney Snow

EPILOGUE

It is an honor to name just a few remarkable women in the Bible who are Daughters of the King:

Eve-The mother of us all, wife to Adam
(Genesis 3:20)

Mary - The Mother of Jesus
(Luke 1; John 2)

Queen Esther - Put her life at risk to save her people (The book of Esther)

Ruth & Naomi - A Beautiful Story of Loyalty
(The Book of Ruth)

Elizabeth - Mother of John the Baptist
(Luke 1)

Rachel - Loved by Jacob and betrayed by her father through deception (Genesis 29)

Hagar - Birthed a baby for Sarah and Abraham (Genesis 16; Genesis 21)

Mary Magdalene - Devoted follower of Jesus
(Luke 8; Mark 16)

Martha - A dedicated servant of Jesus who sat at His feet as he taught (Luke 11)

Rebekah - Birthed the first twins mentioned in the Bible, Jacob and Esau
(Genesis 25: 22-24)

The Shulamite Woman - The Heroine of Solomon
(Song of Songs 1-8)

Queen of Sheba - Embraced Wisdom
(1Kings 10; 2 Chronicles 9)

The Shunamite Woman - Never lost her faith
(2 Kings 4:8; 8:1)

Lydia - Mastered her art by maintaining spiritual beliefs and ethics (Acts 16; 40)

Abigail - A courageous and wise woman of strength who allowed no foolishness
(1 Samuel 25)

Deborah, Judge of Israel – A prophetess with the ability to inspire others to fulfill the call of God on their lives
(Judges 4; Judges 5)

The Proverbs 31 Woman - The virtuous woman (Proverbs 31)

The list can go on and on. Can you name a few?

_____

_____

_____

_____

_____

_____

This book is a tribute to the following women:

- Maya Angelou
- Michelle Obama
- Coretta Scott King
- Winnie Mandela
- Oprah Winfrey
- Toni Morrison
- Terry McMillan
- Eartha Kitt
- Alice Walker
- Joyce Meyers
- Rosa Parks
- Harriet Tubman
- Cicely Tyson
- Whoopi Goldberg
- Yolanda Adams
- Taraji P. Henson
- "Mary Mary" Tina & Erica Campbell
- Tamela Mann
- Barbara Bush
- Nancy Regan
- Beyonce Knowles
- Tina Knowles

- Tina Turner
- Fantasia
- Shirley MacLaine
- Patti LaBelle
- Queen Aretha Franklin
- Shirley Caesar
- Dottie Peoples
- Kelly Price
- Stephanie Mills
- Hillary Clinton
- Angelina Jolie
- Mariah Carey
- Jennifer Lopez
- Demi Moore
- Marilyn Monroe
- Angela Lansbury
- Vickie Winans
- Dr. Juanakee Adams
- Janet Jackson
- Jacqueline Kennedy Onassis
- Beverly Crawford
- Ce Ce Winans
- Ellen DeGeneres

- Nancy Wilson
- Mary McLeod Bethune
- Katherine Jackson
- Sanaa Lathan
- Iyanla Vanzant
- Maxine Waters
- Lena Horne
- Angela Bassett
- Natalie Cole
- Whitney Houston
- Alicia Keys
- Barbara Walters
- Halle Berry
- Camille Cosby
- Anita Baker
- Dianne Carroll
- Kathy Bates
- Alfre Woodard
- Phoebe Snow
- Queen Latifah
- Betty Ford
- Della Reese
- Denise Nicholas

- Gladys Knight
- Debra L. Lee (BET)
- Dionne Warwick
- Jewel Diamond Taylor
- Taffi Dollar
- Mary J. Blige
- Jill Scott
- Barbara Jordan
- Shirley Chisholm
- Josephine Baker
- Maria Shriver
- Sophia Loren
- Ruby Dee
- Susan Taylor
- Diane Youngblood
- Chaka Kahn
- Diana Ross
- Gladys Knight
- Madame C. J. Walker
- Mahalia Jackson
- The Delaney Sisters
- Pam Grier
- Meryl Streep

- Valerie Simpson
- Etta James
- Queen Elizabeth
- Billie Holiday
- Minnie Riperton
- Juanita Bynum
- Sandra Bullock
- Melissa McCarthy
- Condoleezza Rice
- Teena Marie
- Jane Fonda
- Maria Shriver
- Florence Brooks
- Verlon Hurst
- Maisha Robinson, MSW, LCSW
- Dr. Tina Sherrell O'Neal
- Sabrina Nelson
- Sarah Vaughn
- Priscilla Shirer
- Dorothy Porter Evans
- Nellie Porter
- Connie Cunningham
- and many more

I celebrate the following women in my own life:

- My Grandmothers – Mrs. Bertha Mae (Alexander) Perry and Mrs. Rosenia Magnolia (Colvin) McKinney
- Godmother – Ruby Tenney (still alive and well at 97 yrs. old)
- My Aunts – Kathleen, Martha, Bertha, Willie Mae, Blanche, Mary Sue, Thelma

Special Women of God:

- Eula McKinney-thank you for all your spiritual inspiration
- Dorothy Jean McKinney
- First Lady, Debra Hatten
- Mother Evelyn Ware and Missionaries of Mt. Grove Missionary Baptist Church, Childersburg, AL
- Sister Mary Carter of Mt. Olive Baptist Church, Harpersville, AL
- Mother Ruby Hamilton of Spirit and Life Ministries, San Fernando, CA,
- Sister Eddie Taylor of Greater Faith Missionary Baptist Church, Los Angeles, CA
- Sister Diane Davis of Prayer Line to God
- Evangelist Priscilla Perry Gibson

- Faithful Inner Circle of Friends and Associates: Thank you all for being there for me in my time of need. You know who you are.

I love you all. Lord, thank you for family and friends.

Honoring the following notable men, who by the grace of God, planted seeds to create us. We were born of a seed planted by man but came from a woman. We didn't just happen. Without man, there wouldn't be girls who grow to become "women". Celebrating the following male mentors:

- JESUS (The most inspirational man in my life)
- Mr. Henry Keith
- Dr. Martin Luther King
- President Barack Obama
- Bishop T.D. Jakes
- Rev. Creflo Dollar
- Pastor Stephen Hamilton
- President John F. Kennedy
- Pastor Robert Hatten
- Rev. Sidney Bush
- Rev. Kenneth Walker
- Rev. Alvin Walker
- Rev. Jerry Ware
- Evangelist Joel Osteen
- President Nelson Mandela
- Tyler Perry
- Steve Harvey

- Dr. Phillip C. McGraw
- Malcolm X
- James Brown, The Godfather of Soul
- Muhammed Ali
- Stevie Wonder
- Marvin Gaye
- Smokey Robinson
- Michael Jackson
- Fred Hammond
- Marvin Sapp
- Lee Williams
- Derric Brown, MSW
- Denzel Washington
- Sidney Poitier
- Shuan McKinney (The best brother in the world)
- Uncle Thomas Perry
- Robert Russa Moton
- Gary Youngblood
- Quincy Jones
- Sam Cooke

If your name was not mentioned, you're still in my heart and in my mind.

Finally, brothers and sisters,

Whatever is true,

Whatever is noble,

Whatever is right,

Whatever is pure,

Whatever is lovely,

Whatever is admirable...

If anything is excellent or praiseworthy,

Think about such things.

~Philippians 4:8 NIV

Remember, what we focus on the most is what we give strength to. May the God of peace and blessings be with you.

"A Daughter of the King" is a guide to create and maintain a personal and spiritual outlook on life. I look forward to sharing more with you.

PS, I love you.

~Kathleen Patricia Perry McKinney Snow, Author

Kathleen Patricia Perry McKinney Snow

ABOUT THE AUTHOR

Born with an insatiable appetite for knowledge, Kathleen Patricia Perry McKinney Snow took advantage of each opportunity to soar to new heights in her life and career. After completing her undergraduate studies, she worked in medical administration for 20+ years while living in California. After she moved back home to Alabama, Kathleen took on a new venture in the banking field.

A natural-born nurturer, Kathleen frequently visits retirement and convalescent homes. Whether she's reading to or engaging in pleasant conversation with patients, Kathleen extends a helping hand and a smile to those who are sick and shut-in. In addition to her retirement home visits, Kathleen serves as a companion to a retired special education teacher who requires special attention and care.

Since retirement from the workforce, Kathleen has ventured into writing books. She endeavors to inspire her readers through words of wisdom birthed out of her life's experiences.

Made in the USA
Columbia, SC
18 August 2020

15480329R10100